HISTORY IN ART

ISLAMIC EMPIRES

Raintree

Chicago, Illinois

NICOLA BARBER

Originated by Dot Gradations Ltd
Printed and bound in Hong Kong, China,
by South China Printing Company.

09 08 07 06 05
10 9 8 7 6 5 4 3 2 1

Library of Congress Cataloging-in-Publication Data

Barber, Nicola.
  Islamic Empires [sic] / Nicola Barber.
     p. cm. -- (History in art)
  Includes bibliographical references and index.
  ISBN 1-4109-0522-5
  1. Art, Islamic--Juvenile literature. 2. Islamic Empire--Juvenile
literature. I. Title. II. Series.
  N6260.B367 2005
  704'.088297--dc22
                        2004007527

Acknowledgments
The publishers would like to thank the following for permission to
reproduce photographs (t = top, b = bottom): Art Archive pp. 11,
13, 22 (British Library), 27 (Topkapi Museum Istanbul/Dagli Orti), 31
(t) (Dagli Orti), 37 (b), 39 (b), 43 (t) (Dagli Orti); Bonhams, London
pp. 40, 42; Bridgeman Art Library pp. 5 (t), 5 (b) (Lauros/Giraudon),
6 (t), 6 (b), 7, 9 (both), 10 (t) (Ashmolean Museum), 12, 14 (b)
(Index), 14 (t) (Ken Welsh), 15 (Peter Willi), 16 (Giraudon), 18, 19,
20 (t) (Giraudon), 20 (b), 21, 25, 26 (Giraudon), 30, 31 (b), 32, 33
(t), 33 (b) (Giraudon), 34, 35 (both), 36, 39 (t), 41, 45; British Library
p. 24; British Museum p. 10 (b); The Trustees of the Chester Beatty
Library, Dublin p. 43 (b); Corbis pp. 17, 23 (t), 29, 38; Freer Gallery
of Art, Smithsonian Institute p. 28; Harcourt pp. 1, 3, 8, 23 (b), 37 (t),
44. Map on p. 4 is by Encompass Graphics.

Cover photograph of an astrolabe made by Ahmad Ibn Khalaf, an
Iraqi Arab, in the 9th century C.E., reproduced with permission of
Bridgeman.

Every effort has been made to contact copyright holders of any
material reproduced in this book. Any omissions will be rectified in
subsequent printings if notice is given to the publishers.

The publisher would like to thank Venetia Porter of the British
Museum for her assistance in the preparation of this book.

The paper used to print this book comes from sustainable resources.

**Note: When Muslims say the name of one of the prophets,
they always say, "Peace Be Upon Him" afterward. This
phrase is shown in this book as** ﷺ **.**

Contents

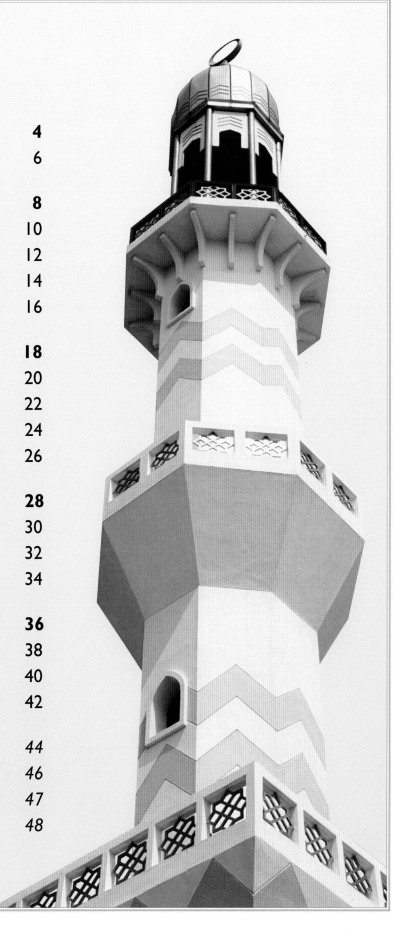

Art as Evidence

This book looks at art over a period of a thousand years—from roughly the 600s to the 1600s—and over an area that stretched from Spain in the west to India in the east. These were the heartlands of an Islamic empire that reached from northwestern Africa to Southeast Asia. The common feature that linked the peoples of this vast region across this span of time was the religion of Islam. With such a wide geographic spread and long history, Islamic art was inevitably shaped by different regional styles and developments through time. Yet the art of Islam, rooted in the Islamic faith, retained its own unique characteristics throughout the centuries.

▼ This map shows shows the extent of the Islamic Empire on three dates during its long history. The locations of the main places mentioned in the text throughout the book are also shown.

The Ka'ba

The Ka'ba (from the Arabic for "cube") is a simple, cube-shaped structure, built of stone blocks. It contains the black stone, a meteorite that is believed to have been sent from heaven to Earth. According to Muslim belief, the Ka'ba was built by Ibrahim and his son Ismail, and pilgrimage to the Ka'ba was well established before the time of Muhammad ﷺ. After the Prophet Muhammad ﷺ cleansed the Ka'ba of idols, it became the sacred shrine of Islam. It has remained the *qibla* (direction of prayer) for Muslims throughout the centuries.

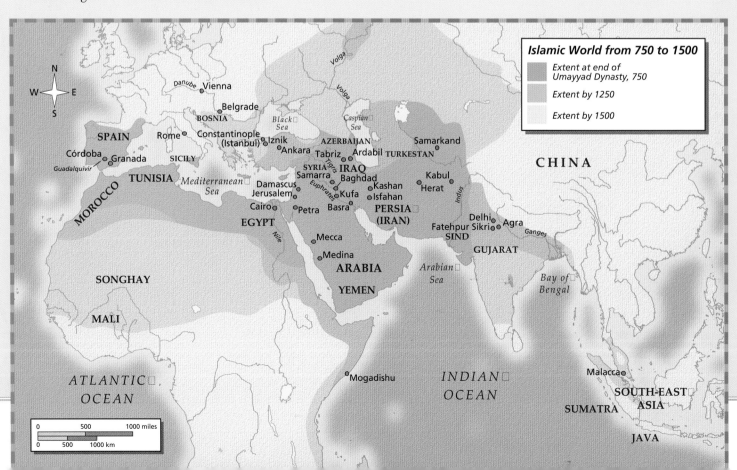

Islamic World from 750 to 1500

- Extent at end of Umayyad Dynasty, 750
- Extent by 1250
- Extent by 1500

N W E S

Volga
Volga
Danube — Vienna
Belgrade
BOSNIA
Black Sea
Caspian Sea
SPAIN   Rome   Constantinople (Istanbul)   Iznik
Córdoba   Granada   SICILY   Ankara   Tabriz   Ardabil   Samarkand   TURKESTAN
Guadalquivir   AZERBAIJAN
SYRIA   Tigris   IRAQ
TUNISIA   Mediterranean Sea   Samarra   Baghdad   Kabul
MOROCCO   Damascus   Euphrates   Kashan   Herat   Indus
Jerusalem   Kufa   Isfahan
Cairo   Petra   Basra   PERSIA (IRAN)   CHINA
EGYPT   Nile   Delhi   Agra
Fatehpur Sikri   Ganges
Mecca   SIND
Medina   GUJARAT
ARABIA   Arabian Sea   Bay of Bengal
SONGHAY   YEMEN

MALI

ATLANTIC OCEAN   Mogadishu   INDIAN OCEAN   Malacca
SOUTH-EAST ASIA
SUMATRA

JAVA

0   500   1000 miles
0   500   1000 km

Islam arose in the 600s, in Mecca (in present-day Saudi Arabia). A merchant named Muhammad ﷺ received a series of revelations, or messages, from Allah. The messages said that Allah was the one God. At the time, most people in Arabia worshiped many gods and idols. Muhammad ﷺ preached this message and converted people to Islam, meaning "submission to the will of Allah."

The flight to Medina

Many people in Mecca were unhappy about Islam. In 622 the Prophet Muhammad ﷺ and his followers, known as Muslims, left Mecca for Yathrib, a city about 250 miles (400 kilometers) to the north. This city was Muhammad's home for the rest of his life, and was renamed Medina, or "City of the Prophet." Muhammad ﷺ died in 632, having conquered Mecca and destroyed the idols at the shrine called the **Ka'ba**.

The birth of Islamic art

The new religion spread quickly across Arabia during Muhammad's ﷺ lifetime. It continued to spread after his death as his followers conquered neighboring lands. The Muslims defeated the armies of the **Byzantine** and the **Sassanian** (Persian) Empires. They took control of their lands, including areas that are the modern-day countries of Syria, Azerbaijan, Afghanistan, Iraq, and Iran. It was this expansion that drew together the ingredients for the birth of Islamic art. The Byzantines and the Persians had highly developed traditions of art and architecture. It was these influences, coupled with the beliefs of the new Islamic faith, that led to the development of a distinctive Islamic art.

▶ The *mihrab* in the mosque of Sheik Lutfallah in Isfahan, Iran, shows some of the distinctive characteristics of Islamic art.

The mihrab indicates the direction of prayer, the qibla, for worshippers in the mosque.

This three-dimensional Islamic decoration is known as muqarnas.

Calligraphy is used as surface ornamentation around the mihrab.

Glazed tiles decorate every surface of the interior of the mosque.

The Development of Islamic Art

As the Islamic world expanded, Islamic art and architecture flourished. Styles of architecture developed for important buildings such as mosques, **madrasahs** (Islamic colleges), and palaces. Other arts included metalwork, painting, ceramic pottery, and the making of tiles, textiles, and carpets. Looking at objects and asking who made them, who they were made for, and why they were made, gives us a glimpse of life in the Islamic empires.

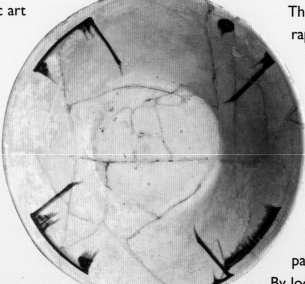

► This ceramic bowl from eastern Iran is dated from the 800s to the 900s.

The Islamic faith spread rapidly during the 600s and the 700s. By 750, the Islamic world stretched from Spain in the west to Afghanistan in the east. In the following centuries, local rulers established dynasties and empires in various parts of the Islamic world. By looking at buildings and artifacts from these empires, we can see that many features of Islamic art were used throughout the Islamic world. Yet each empire also had its own distinctive style, depending on where it was, when it was at the height of its power, and what the culture of its people was like.

◄ This painting comes from the *Akbarnama (The History of Akbar)*, and dates from the 1590s. The book was commissioned by the **Mughal** emperor Akbar (ruled 1556–1605) and tells the story of his life. Illustrations such as these can give huge amounts of detailed information about the lives of the Mughal emperors. In the background we see the Red Fort, a structure that Akbar built when he moved his capital from Delhi to Agra in 1557.

This is the Yamuna River.

Akbar himself is shown taming the savage elephant Hawa'i.

The Akbarnama *was written by Akbar's close friend, Abu Fazl, and was illustrated by painters in the royal studios.*

Many Islamic rulers were enthusiastic and knowledgeable patrons of the arts and sciences. They encouraged scholars from all over the Islamic world to come to their courts and set up workshops for the production of carpets, pottery, or metalwork. Some of the artists and craftworkers became famous for their work, including the Baghdad calligrapher Ibn al-Bawwab and the **Ottoman** architect Sinan.

Examining the evidence

The history of Islamic coins provides an interesting glimpse of life in early Islamic times. When the Muslims first conquered the **Byzantine** and **Sassanian** empires, they continued to use the local currencies. These coins were stamped with the busts of Byzantine or Sassanian emperors and used the Greek and Persian languages. Gradually, the new Arab rulers started to change the coins a little bit at a time.

It was the **Umayyad caliph** Abd al-Malik who decided to overhaul the whole system. In 696, he introduced a new Islamic coinage. In line with Islamic tradition (see page 9), the coins contained no images. Instead, the coins showed the *Shahada,* the Muslim profession of belief in God, and a date. Islamic coins also often carried the name of the place where they were made, and the ruler under whom they were minted. In daily life, these coins reminded everyone of the power of Islam and of their Muslim rulers.

How has Islamic architecture survived?

The earliest Islamic building to have survived in its original form is the Dome of the Rock in Jerusalem (see page 8), although it has been restored over the centuries. From Spain to India, many other buildings still stand as evidence of the Islamic empires that once held sway. However, some buildings have long been demolished or have disappeared under newer construction. For example, nothing remains of the spectacular circular city of Baghdad. Founded in 762–763 as the capital of the **Abbasid** Empire, it was destroyed by the **Mongols** in 1258 (see page 18), and its ruins lie beneath the modern-day city. For information about these sites, we rely on historical descriptions and, where possible, on archaeology.

▼ The coin from early Umayyad times has verses from the Qur'an stating the oneness of God, the essence of the Islamic faith.

The Spread of Islam

After the death of the Prophet Muhammad ﷺ in 632, the leadership of the Islamic community passed in turn to four successors, or **caliphs**, known by many Muslims as the *Rashidun*—the "judicious ones." The last was Ali ﷺ, cousin of the Prophet Muhammad ﷺ and therefore the only caliph to be directly related to him. His appointment was the start of a long-lasting division within the Islamic world.

Most Muslims believed that the caliph should be the person best able to uphold the customs and traditions (the **Sunnah**) of Islam; these people became known as **Sunni** Muslims. Others believed that only someone from the same family as Muhammad ﷺ should become caliph; they became known as **Shi'ite** Muslims. In 661, Ali ﷺ was murdered, and the governor of Syria, Mu'awiya, seized power. This began the **Umayyad** dynasty—when Mu'awiya died, the title of caliph passed to his son. The Umayyads expanded the Islamic Empire both westward and eastward.

▼ Inside the Dome of the Rock in Jerusalem, the sacred rock is enclosed by a circle of pillars that support the mosque's dome.

The Dome of the Rock

The oldest surviving Muslim building, the Dome of the Rock in Jerusalem, is also one of the most sacred sites in the Islamic world. Arab armies had captured Jerusalem in 638. Work on the mosque began under the Umayyad caliph, Abd al-Malik, in 685, and was completed in 691. It was built over the rock on Mount Zion from where Muslims believe Muhammad ﷺ went up to Allah on the "**Night of Ascent**." The construction of the Dome of the Rock sent a powerful message to members of the Jewish and Christian faiths, for whom Jerusalem is also a holy city. The mosque was built on the site of the old Jewish temple. Inscriptions from the **Qur'an** that adorn the walls take issue with some aspects of Christian belief.

The upper half of the walls are covered with tiles that date from the time of the **Ottoman** sultan, Suleiman (see page 26).

The outer shape of the building is an octagon.

A panel decorated with words from the Qur'an runs around the building.

The lower half of the walls is covered with marble.

The Great Mosque

The Great Mosque of Damascus was started by the Umayyad caliph al-Walid in 705 and was completed ten years later. It was a hugely expensive project, designed to create a prestigious place of worship in the Umayyad capital. The mosque was built on the site of a Roman temple that the **Byzantines** had converted into a Christian church. It is a large rectangular building with a courtyard to one side, and it provided a model for the construction of other mosques in the early Islamic world.

◀ Beautiful mosaics decorate some of the outside walls of the Great Mosque of Damascus. This mosaic is on the end of the prayer hall.

The mosaics depict trees and buildings, but there are no human figures.

The style of the mosaics points to the influence of Byzantine and Christian art.

The mosaics may represent images of Paradise or may celebrate Umayyad conquests.

Idols and images

One striking aspect of the mosaics that decorate both the Dome of the Rock and the Great Mosque of Damascus is that no living beings are represented. There is no specific wording in the Qur'an that forbids the practice. However, it became the tradition very early in Islamic history to avoid the depiction of living things in mosques and other religious buildings, such as *madrasahs* and tombs. It was thought that the representation of figures might lead people to worship idols, as had been the practice before the time of Muhammadﷺ. It was also believed that the creation of living forms was unique to God. Nevertheless, pictures of people and animals often appeared in secular (nonreligious) settings such as palaces, as well as on books, pottery, and metalwork.

A detail from the mosaics that decorate the Great Mosque of Damascus.

This mosaic used plantlike patterns.

Mosaic is made from small pieces of glass.

9

The Abbasids

The **Abbasids** came to power in 750, after seizing control from the **Umayyads**. They moved the capital of the Islamic Empire from Damascus to Iraq, establishing a new capital city in Baghdad in 762–763. The peak of the Abbasid Empire came during the reign of **Caliph** Harun al-Rashid (786–809), who ruled over a court of great ceremony and opulence. His court was the setting for the tales that make up the *Thousand and One Nights,* although they were not collected and written down until much later.

▶ This lusterware bowl dates from the 800s and was made in Samarra, in Iraq. It has a shiny **luster** glaze. Such pottery was made to satisfy the Abbasid court's demands for luxury ware.

▼ This fragment is part of a reconstruction of a wall painting from the Jawsaq al-Khaqani palace in Samarra. The palace was the residence of the caliph during the time that the Abbasids inhabited Samarra as their capital.

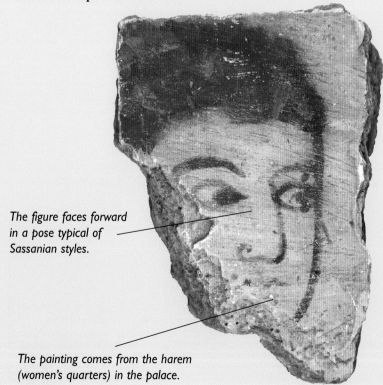

The figure faces forward in a pose typical of Sassanian styles.

The painting comes from the harem (women's quarters) in the palace.

Looking east

During the excavation of an Abbasid palace in Samarra, beginning in 1911, fragments of a wall painting were discovered. The image shows two women dancers pouring wine, and it decorated a wall in the **harem** (women's quarters) of the palace. The style shows the influence of **Sassanian** art from the Persian Empire conquered by the Muslims in the 600s. It underlines the increasing importance of Persian influences in the Islamic Empire after the Abbasids moved the capital eastward. As a result of this move, the Abbasids distanced themselves from Arabia and the traditional heartland of Islam. They relied on Persian bureaucrats to run the empire and Persian troops to defend them. Like the earlier Sassanian rulers, the Abbasid caliphs lived in opulent imperial style, very different from the simple, religious lives of the Prophet Muhammad ﷺ and the *Rashidun.*

Samarra

In about 836, unrest in Baghdad between the local population and Turkish troops in the **Abbasid** army drove the Abbasids to abandon their capital and move 60 miles (90 kilometers) north to Samarra. The Abbasids stayed there for just over 50 years, returning to Baghdad in 892. A new city quickly developed at Samarra, stretching some 20 miles (30 kilometers) along the Tigris River. Under Caliph al-Mutawakkil (ruled 847–861), huge building works were undertaken, including the Great Mosque and many lavish palaces. Building work stopped when the Abbasids returned to Baghdad, and much of the population left the city. Archaeologists have found Samarra to be a rich source of information about Islamic art. It was inhabited for a very short period, allowing them to accurately date styles of pottery and carving.

▶ The Great Mosque in Samarra, built between 849 and 851, was the biggest in the Islamic world. Outside the main courtyard stood a conical **minaret** with a spiral ramp winding around its outside.

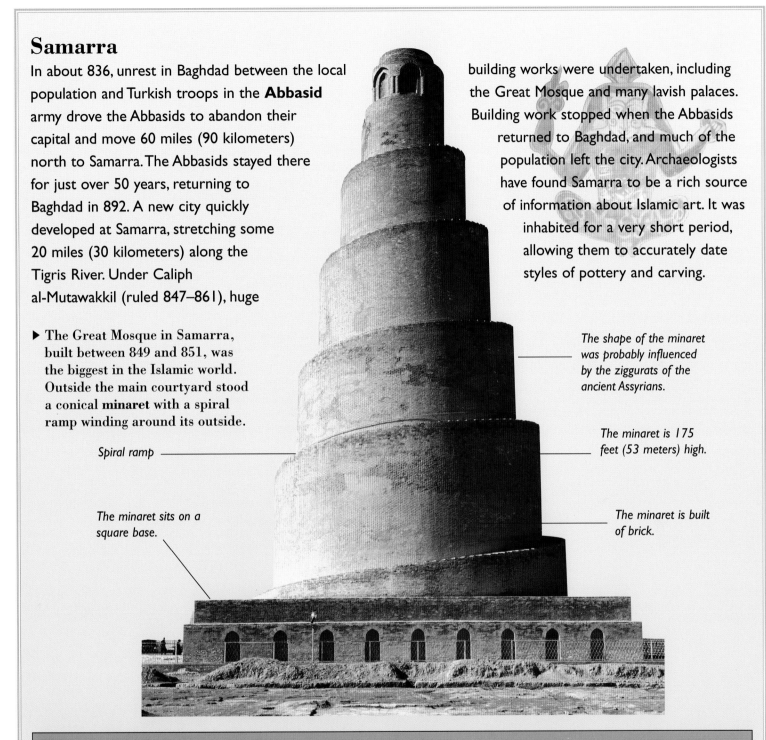

Spiral ramp

The minaret sits on a square base.

The shape of the minaret was probably influenced by the ziggurats of the ancient Assyrians.

The minaret is 175 feet (53 meters) high.

The minaret is built of brick.

The round city

The second Abbasid caliph, al-Mansur (ruled 754–775), built Baghdad at the meeting point of several important trade routes. The city quickly became a commercial hub. Nothing remains today of the original city of Baghdad—much was destroyed by the **Mongols** in 1258, and the remainder has been built over.

We know from descriptions that Baghdad was a circular city, with the caliph's imposing royal palace and a large mosque in the middle. The symbolic message of this design was clear. The caliph was at the center of the Islamic world and far removed from ordinary Muslims.

Architecture

The most basic and most typical type of architecture found throughout the Islamic world was a house with a courtyard. Such houses were suited to the hot climates of most Islamic countries. They also reflected the culture of Islamic societies, in which women were shielded from the outside world, and the privacy of the family was highly valued. This emphasis on the inside space, rather than the outside, is seen in architecture throughout the Islamic world. There are certain architectural features that are found all over the Islamic world. Some, such as the **minaret**, the **mihrab**, and the **minbar**, are particular features of a mosque.

Main features

Other features, such as domes, courtyards, and arches, are found in all types of buildings. In central Asia and Persia, a typical feature was the *iwan*, an open-air hall with an arched ceiling. This came originally from the **Sassanians** and was used in mosques, *madrasahs* (Islamic colleges), **caravanserais**, and tombs.

▼ This is the courtyard of the Friday mosque in Isfahan, looking towards the *iwan*. There are four *iwans* in the huge courtyard, one on each side. This layout became common in mosques and *madrasahs* in central Asia.

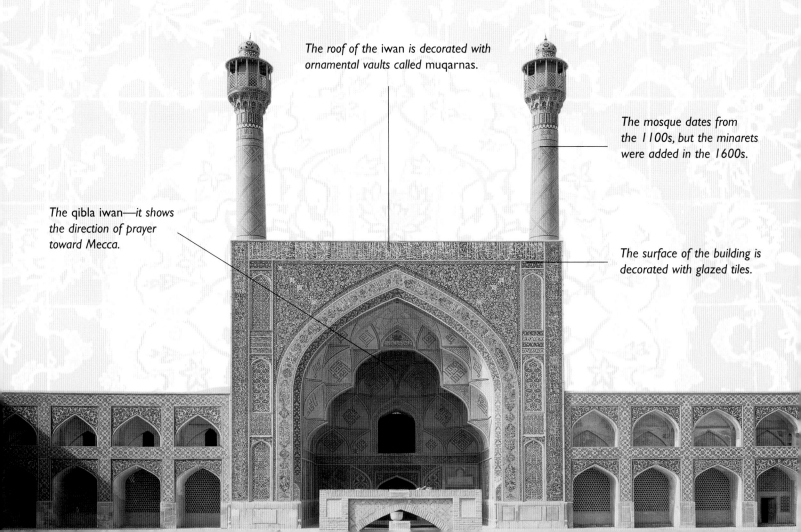

The roof of the iwan *is decorated with ornamental vaults called* muqarnas.

The mosque dates from the 1100s, but the minarets were added in the 1600s.

The qibla iwan—*it shows the direction of prayer toward Mecca.*

The surface of the building is decorated with glazed tiles.

In their buildings, Islamic architects aimed to create a sense of weightlessness and light. This was achieved partly by the use of extensive decoration on every surface. Mosaics reflected light, and carved stonework cut away the heaviness of supporting walls. These helped to create the feeling of airiness that is the hallmark of some of the greatest Islamic architectural triumphs.

Types of buildings

A mosque was a basic requirement for any Muslim community. Mosques, ranging from small local mosques to the large communal Friday mosques used for the main service of the week, were built everywhere in the Islamic world.

The construction of tombs in the Islamic world was more controversial, because the glorification of the dead was not part of Islamic tradition. Nevertheless, from the time of the **Seljuks** (990–1118), wealthy rulers constructed **mausoleums** in preparation for their deaths. Many Islamic rulers built large complexes, often including a mosque and a *madrasah*. *Madrasahs* were places of learning where students studied the Islamic religion and Islamic law. Many **Sunni** *madrasahs* were founded by the Seljuks, partly in reaction to the threat from the **Shi'ite Fatimids** in Egypt (see page 16).

◀ This is the funerary complex of the Mamluk sultan Qa'itbay (reigned 1468–1496). It contained a *madrasah*, a mosque, the tomb of Qa'itbay, a hospice, and a source of clean water.

Al-Andalus

When the **Abbasids** took power, the first action of the new **caliph** was to massacre members of the **Umayyad** clan in order to secure his authority over the Islamic Empire. But an Umayyad prince named Abd al-Rahman escaped. He made his way across North Africa to Spain, where he defeated the Abbasid ruler in 756. He established an independent Islamic state, called al-Andalus, in southern Spain. By the 900s, it had become a renowned center for learning and the arts.

▲ This magnificent dome was added to the Great Mosque of Córdoba in the 900s. A glittering mosaic decorates the interior of the dome. It is made from gold cubes that were brought from the Byzantine Empire.

The Great Mosque at Córdoba

Abd al-Rahman founded a dynasty that ruled over al-Andalus for nine generations. He made his capital at Córdoba, on the north bank of the Guadalquivir River. There he began to construct a mosque that would be large enough for all of the city's Muslim citizens to meet for prayer. He also started other construction projects including palaces, mosques, bathhouses, gardens, and fountains. Córdoba became one of the most celebrated cities in the Islamic world.

◄ This is the interior of the Great Mosque in Córdoba. The double arches were inspired by the arches of the Great Mosque in Damascus, and possibly also by Roman aqueducts in Spain.

The double arches were used to raise the height of the roof.

The upper arches are supported by short piers.

The red color in the arches is brick, and the white is stone. The contrast is made greater with paint.

The lower arches rest on columns.

By constructing the Great Mosque, Abd al-Rahman and his successors tried to recreate the splendors lost to the Umayyads in Syria. The mosque was built from 784 to 786, but it was enlarged three times over subsequent centuries. Craftworkers came from afar to work on the mosque—not from the main Islamic Empire (under the control of the Abbasid enemy at the time), but from Christian Constantinople (remaining under the rule of the **Byzantines**). The Umayyads maintained good relations with the Byzantines, as they largely did with the Christian and Jewish populations in al-Andalus. These groups were tolerated as long as they did not rebel against their Muslim rulers.

Palace splendors

The Umayyad Dynasty reached its peak in al-Andalus under the rule of Abd al-Rahman III (912–961), who proclaimed himself caliph in 929. He founded a new capital just outside Córdoba, called Madinat al-Zahra. It had a palace, government offices, and housing for up to 20,000 staff. Only ruins survive of Madinat al-Zahra, but the splendor of life at the Spanish Umayyad court can be glimpsed through the exquisite carved ivory caskets that were a favorite of wealthy courtiers. The ivory was from Africa and came from elephant and hippopotamus tusks. These caskets were used to store jewelry or perfumes. Their decoration often included figures and animals as well as inscriptions stating the name of the owner.

The Alhambra

The rule of the Umayyads in Spain was replaced in the 1000s by the **Almoravid** and **Almohad Berber** dynasties. At the same time, the Christian reconquest of Spain began. By the end of the 1200s, the only remaining Muslim stronghold was Granada. The rulers of Granada, the Nasrids, lived in a fortified palace called the Alhambra, built between 1238 and 1358. Today, it is one of the best-preserved palaces of the Islamic world. Like the Topkapi Sarai in Istanbul (see page 26), its layout reflects the Islamic preference for a mazelike collection of courts and rooms rather than a grand, balanced design similar to that seen in many European palaces. The Alhambra contains some exquisite stone carving as well as beautiful gardens.

The inscription tells us that the casket was presented to al-Mughira in 968.

The central figure is playing an ud—a lute.

This figure is holding a fan.

This figure is holding a bottle and a flower on a long stalk.

The lions beneath the figures symbolize royalty.

▶ This casket was made for al-Mughira, son of Abd al-Rahman III.

The Fatimids

By the 900s, the **Abbasid caliph** had been reduced to little more than a figurehead, as rival groups seized power in various parts of the Islamic world. The **Seljuk** Turks, who converted to Islam in the 990s, seized power from the Abbasids in the 1000s. In 969, the **Fatimids** defeated the Abbasid rulers in Egypt, and in 973 established their capital at al-Qahirah, "the triumphant"—known as Cairo in English. Unlike the Abbasids and Seljuks, who were **Sunni** Muslims, the Fatimids were **Shi'ites**, and their leader claimed descent from Fatimah, daughter of the Prophet Muhammad ﷺ.

Wealth and prosperity

The Fatimid Empire was very prosperous because of the wealth from Egyptian agriculture and Egypt's position at the center of the profitable trade between the Mediterranean and lands to the east. This prosperity was reflected in the opulence of the **Fatimid** court. The Fatimid rulers surrounded themselves with beautiful pottery, glass, metalwork, and other objects such as this ewer made from rock crystal. Many of these objects were made in the workshops of al-Fustat, old Cairo. Fatimid craftworkers became renowned for their creativity and skills. Cairo soon rivaled Baghdad as a cultural and artistic center.

▶ This ewer, made from rock crystal, dates from the 900s. Rock crystal was imported to Egypt from Arabia, Iraq, and East Africa. It was used to make glasses, ewers, and basins for holding liquids. The purity of rock crystal also reminded Muslims of words in the Qur'an that refer to the crystal cups that true believers used for drinking in Paradise.

Rock crystal was highly prized because it was supposed to shatter if it came into contact with poison—the person using it could trust that the drink was safe.

The crystal was hollowed out to make ewers and other vessels and then carved on the outside.

Shi'ite Islam

When the Fatimids founded Cairo, they built a large mosque called al-Azhar, or "the splendid." This mosque became a center of learning and is still a university today. During the Fatimid period it was the focus for the teaching of Shi'ite Islam. While the Fatimids waged war on the Sunni Abbasids, they also attempted to convert Abbasid subjects to Shi'ite Islam. They did this through the use of *da'is* (missionaries). Al-Azhar became a training center for *da'is*. However, despite this program of conversion, Sunni Islam remained widespread. However, Saladin seized power in 1169 and two years later proclaimed a return to Sunni Islam in Egypt.

The Fatimid Treasury

What evidence do we have today of life at the Fatimid court? In fact, very little, since the Fatimid palaces have disappeared. Many of the sumptuous objects made during the period have been destroyed. During the 1000s, there was famine and political unrest in Egypt. The Great Treasury, where the Fatimids stored their most precious objects, was repeatedly looted between 1067 and 1072. Many objects were smashed, sold, or melted down. Luckily, two detailed descriptions of the Great Treasury survive, giving us a glimpse of the huge and priceless collection of the caliph. One description lists 36,000 items made of rock crystal.

▼ This view looks down into the courtyard of the al-Azhar mosque in Cairo, Egypt.

The mosque has two **minarets**.

The dome was built in the 1100s.

The mosque was founded in 970; the facade of the courtyard was added later.

The Great Empires

The **Mongols** were **nomads** who came from the steppes of central Asia. In 1206, they formed a confederation of tribes under a leader called Genghis Khan (ruled 1206–1227). The Mongols first attacked China, before turning their attentions to the Islamic lands to the west. In 1258, Genghis's grandson Hulagu sacked Baghdad, finally bringing the rule of the **Abbasid caliphs** to an end. It was the first time that the Islamic world had been overwhelmed by non-Muslims. The Mongols wreaked havoc as they conquered, leaving a trail of death and destruction behind them.

Conversion and reconstruction

In the years following the sack of Baghdad, the Mongol khan (emperor) converted to Islam. By the beginning of the 1300s, many Mongols had followed his example and adopted Islam. The Mongols began a process of reconstruction, rebuilding the cities they had destroyed in even more splendid architectural styles than before. They also became great patrons of the arts and sciences, encouraging poetry, painting, and the studies of astronomy and history.

▶ This illustration is taken from a book by Rashid al-Din. It shows the Mongol leader Genghis Khan in battle.

18

The *Jami al-Tawarikh (World History)* of Rashid al-Din was produced in Tabriz, Iran, in the early 1300s. Rashid al-Din was vizier (chief minister) to the Mongol khan Ghazan. He was also a historian. His book included not only an account of the Prophet Muhammad ﷺ and his followers, but also of the Jews, the Chinese, the Indians, and the Turkish and Mongol tribes. Several copies were made and illustrated, in both the Arabic and Persian languages. The Mongol patronage of such work showed their desire to mark their own place in history and in the Islamic world.

Samarkand splendor

By the middle of the 1300s, Mongol power was fading. Timur, the last Mongol conqueror, attempted to reverse this decline. From the 1380s until his death in 1405, Timur established control over much of central Asia, Iran, and Iraq, capturing Delhi, India, in the east and

Timur the Lame (c.1336–1405)

Timur (known as "the Lame") was born near Samarkand and claimed descent from Genghis Khan. He was determined to bring the Islamic world under **Mongol** rule, and set about this task with great ruthlessness. It is said that in 1387, after his defeat of Isfahan, a tower of 70,000 human skulls was erected to deter any would-be opponents. In 1398 he invaded India, sacking Delhi and massacring its inhabitants. Nevertheless, Timur was a devout Muslim and a great patron of arts and architecture. During his lifetime and after his death, he captured the imagination of Muslims and non-Muslims alike. In the 1500s, the English playwright Christopher Marlowe wrote a play about him, *Tamburlaine the Great.*

Ankara (in modern-day Turkey) in the west. He made his capital at Samarkand, and took back wealth, scholars, and craftworkers from all over his newly conquered empire. The results of Timur's patronage of art and architecture can be seen today in buildings such as the Gur-i Amir.

▼ Timur himself was buried in the Gur-i Amir, although the tomb was originally built for one of his grandsons. The inside of the Gur-i Amir tomb uses materials of great richness for decoration, including alabaster, onyx, marble, jasper, and gold.

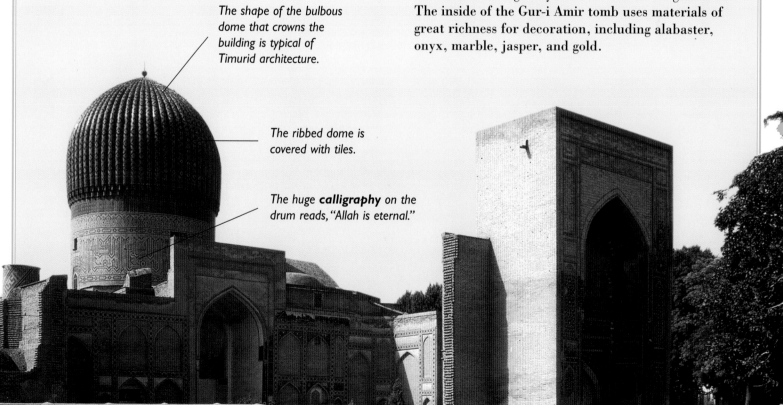

The shape of the bulbous dome that crowns the building is typical of Timurid architecture.

The ribbed dome is covered with tiles.

*The huge **calligraphy** on the drum reads, "Allah is eternal."*

The Safavids

The **Safavids** came originally from Azerbaijan, near the Caspian Sea. They took their name from their founder, Safi al-Din. They established their rule in 1501, when they captured Tabriz, and quickly extended their empire across Iran and into Iraq. The Safavids were **Shi'ite** Muslims, who, throughout their rule, battled against their **Sunni** Muslim neighbors for territory—the **Ottoman**s to the west and the **Uzbeks** to the northeast.

▲ This painting of Shah Abbas I dates from the 1600s and comes from **Mughal** India.

The Ardabil carpet

The most famous and successful of the Safavid rulers was Shah Abbas I (reigned 1588–1629), also known as Abbas the Great. He established the Safavid capital at Isfahan, and encouraged the production of superb textiles, carpets, and pottery. Shah Abbas intended that such industries would provide the basis for the prosperity of the Safavid Empire. Isfahan soon became a commercial center, with merchants from all parts of the world visiting the city. There was already a long tradition of carpet weaving in the region, but Shah Abbas established large workshops for the production of high-quality carpets. The carpets varied in size from small prayer rugs to huge carpets, and many were intended for export.

▼ This carpet dates from 1539–1540. It is known as the Ardabil carpet because it was probably made for the Safavid shrine in Ardabil.

The inscription on the carpet reads: "Except for thy heaven, there is no refuge for me in this world. Other than here there is no place for my head. Work of a servant of the court, Maqsud of Kashan, 946.'"

The carpet is made from wool and silk, measuring 36 x 17 feet (10.9 x 5.3 meters).

Mosque lamps hang from the central star of the pattern.

The carpet has 300–325 knots per sq. in. (46–50 per sq. cm), making possible the fine detail of the pattern.

Isfahan

The reconstruction of Isfahan as the new capital of the Safavid Empire (the previous capital was at Tabriz) started in 1597. The city was a tribute to the commercial and military policies of Shah Abbas. Under his rule, the economy of the empire was flourishing, and its borders were secure from the Uzbeks and Ottomans. At the time, Isfahan was one of the largest cities in the world, with a population of about one million people. The majestic buildings in the city impressed visitors, as did the streets lined with plane trees, the canals and parks, and the huge **bazaar**—a center for trade that covered 12 square miles (30 square kilometers). At the center of the city was the Maydan-i Shah, a large public square that formed the heart of the city. It provided space for markets, polo games, and ceremonial occasions.

Riza-i Abbasi (d.1635)

Painting flourished at the Abbasid court, and the leading painter of the early 1600s was Riza-i Abbasi. Some of his paintings were book illustrations, and others were collected into loose-leaf albums. Because of their origins as **nomads**, the Safavids prized portable possessions, and thus were great lovers of books. Riza-i Abbasi developed a new style of painting that was far more naturalistic, or lifelike, than anything seen before. He not only painted refined courtly figures but also ordinary people such as soldiers, peasants, and musicians.

▼ This picture shows the southern end of the great public space in Isfahan, called the Maydan-i Shah.

This is the entrance to the Shah Mosque.

This is the Maydan-i Shah.

This is the qibla **iwan**.

This is the courtyard of the Shah Mosque.

The Maydan-i Shah was lined with shops.

The Mughals

The word "**Mughal**" is a form of "**Mongol**." The first Mughal ruler, Babur (emperor 1526–1530), traced his descent back to both Genghis Khan and Timur. Babur invaded India in the early 1500s, establishing an empire that at its height in the 1500s and 1600s covered the whole country except for the southernmost tip. We know a great deal about the lives of Babur and the other great Mughal emperors from detailed miniature paintings. The Mughals were also responsible for some spectacular buildings, including Akbar's city, Fatehpur Sikri, and the Taj Mahal, built by Shah Jahan.

A vision of paradise

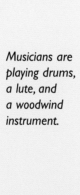

Babur was a brilliant leader and general. He spent much of his life on the battlefield, but he nevertheless found time to write poetry and his memoirs, called the *Babur-nama*. These memoirs were later illustrated by painters who worked in studios at the Mughal court. Paintings in the *Babur-nama* reveal Babur's love of gardens. He created beautiful, formal gardens, where water ran along straight channels and played gently in fountains. The sound and sight of running water was highly prized in Islamic gardens, partly because of the hot, dry climate of much of the Islamic world. Fountains and rivers are also frequently mentioned in the **Qur'an** as a vision of paradise. After his death in 1530, Babur was buried in his favorite garden in Kabul, Afghanistan.

▼ This illustration comes from the *Babur-nama (The History of Babur)*, memoirs that were completed in about 1589. Akbar commissioned the illustrations for his grandfather's memoirs. This painting shows nobles being entertained in a beautiful garden.

Babur sits on a carpet beneath a canopy.

Musicians are playing drums, a lute, and a woodwind instrument.

At the center of the garden is a fountain.

A dancer provides entertainment.

Akbar the Great

Although Babur established the Mughal Empire in India, it was his grandson Akbar (reigned 1556–1605) who extended and secured it. Akbar was fascinated by other religions and adopted a policy of tolerance towards all faiths in his empire. Evidence of Akbar's interests can be seen at Fatehpur Sikri, the new capital city that he built. The style of the buildings at Fatehpur Sikri combined Muslim domes, arches, and courts with traditional Hindu designs. At the center of the city was the *Diwan-i-Khas*—the hall of private audience. In this small pavilion, Akbar would sit and debate with religious scholars. Fatehpur Sikri was abandoned in the 1580s, but the buildings still stand today.

Fatehpur Sikri was built on a ridge overlooking the surrounding countryside.

Walkways from the central throne connect it to the screened balcony.

A central pillar inside the Diwan-i-Khas supports a raised throne.

The whole city was built from red sandstone

▲ This small pavilion is the *Diwan-i-Khas* (the hall of private audience) at Fatehpur Sikri in India. It was built for Akbar in the 1500s.

A monument to love

The Taj Mahal was built by the Mughal emperor Shah Jahan (reigned 1627–1658) as a tomb for his beloved wife Mumtaz Mahal. She died in 1631, giving birth to their fifteenth child. The Taj Mahal is evidence of the huge wealth of the Mughal emperors, who could afford the finest craftspeople and materials from all over the Islamic world for their building projects. Craftspeople from Turkey, Afghanistan, Persia, and central Asia worked on the Taj Mahal, alongside Muslim and Hindu workers from the Mughal Empire itself.

Painting

The art of painting was one of the glories of the Islamic empires. Secular paintings were used to illustrate books (although no images were used to decorate the **Qur'an**), and were therefore often miniature in size and exquisitely detailed. The first illustrated books date from the 1100s, but very few examples survive today. Illustrations were used in the translations made from Greek works and other sources, but the first major flowering of the art of painting happened in Persia in the 1300s.

Persian painting

During the 1300s, the **Mongol** Empire stretched from the Middle East to the Far East. The links between Persia and China encouraged a new style of painting. The *Shahnama*—a long poem recounting the adventures of the Persian kings—was a favorite for illustration. Another work that became very popular was the *Khamseh (Five Poems)* of Nizami. An illustration made in the **Safavid** court for one of the *Khamseh* marks an important break in Islamic tradition. It portrays the ascent of Muhammad ﷺ to the heavens on the **Night of Ascent** (see page 8). The figure of the Prophet is represented, although his face is veiled so that his features cannot be seen.

▶ This illustration comes from a copy of the *Khamseh (Five Poems)* of Nizami. The book was illustrated from 1539 to 1543 for the Safavid ruler, Shah Tahmasp.

These are verses from Nizami's poem.

The illustration shows a musician, Barbad, playing the lute to an Iranian prince, Khusraw.

24

The Ottomans

The **Ottoman** sultans (see pages 26–27) set up a royal studio of painters in Istanbul, with artists from all parts of the empire. The painters brought with them a wide range of styles and expertise. Accounts of Sultan Suleiman's campaigns were illustrated with paintings full of realistic detail, as well as bird's-eye view maps of places such as Lepanto, Genoa, and Venice. In the 1550s, Suleiman ordered the creation of a history of the Ottomans in five volumes. The fifth, the *Suleimannama,* dealt with his own reign, and was completed in 1588. The elegance with which the court painters depicted their subjects marked a new stage in the development of the Ottoman miniature.

The Mughals

The Mughal emperors Akbar, Jahangir, and Shah Jahan took a great interest in miniature painting and had a large royal studio, as at the Ottoman court in Istanbul. Illustrations were made for histories of the Mughals, as well as portraits of the emperors themselves. Jahangir took a particular interest in nature. Because of this, there are many exquisite illustrations of animals from the time of his reign, including zebras, elephants, exotic birds, and horses.

▼ This zebra was painted for the Mughal emperor Jahangir by one of his favorite court painters, Mansur, in 1621. The zebra was brought to the Mughal court from Abyssinia (modern-day Ethiopia).

The Ottomans

The **Ottomans** were descended from nomadic tribes in Anatolia. They established their empire in the region where Europe meets Asia, in what is now Turkey. In 1453, the Ottomans captured Constantinople from the **Byzantines** and made it the capital of their empire, renaming it Istanbul. In 1514, the Ottomans defeated the **Safavids** at Chaldiran and temporarily captured the Safavid capital, Tabriz. In the west, the greatest of the Ottoman sultans, Suleiman "the Magnificent" (reigned 1520–1566), extended Ottoman power across Hungary, threatening both Vienna and Rome with his formidable armies.

This painting can be found at the Topkapi Sarai, the sultan's grand palace in Istanbul (now a museum). It shows the siege of Belgrade in 1521, with the brightly colored tents of the Ottoman army on the right, and the besieged city on the left. Suleiman sits in splendor in his tent while members of the Janissary troops can be seen below, recognizable from their tall hats with a fold of cloth dangling from the back. Some of these highly respected troops were Christian youths. They had been selected to become Muslims, and to receive a strict, thorough education until the age of 25, when they joined the Janissary forces.

◄ This illustration, painted by an artist named Lokman, comes from the *Hunernama*, one of the finest illustrated works containing historical paintings from the **Ottoman** era. It dates from 1588.

Suleiman sits in his tent.

The Ottomans used cannons to bombard the city.

Janissary troops are recognizable by their hats, signs of their obedience to a holy person named Hajji Bektash.

The Ottoman court

The Ottomans had an extremely efficient state bureaucracy that ran all aspects of the empire. The sultan stood at the head of the state with absolute authority. Beneath him, the bureaucracy was divided into three areas: the imperial council and treasury, the military, and the Muslim legal system.

There was a strict hierarchy, and it was often possible to tell the rank and even occupation of a person from his dress. The sultans and their courtiers wore magnificent caftans, often made from silk. On their heads, they wore large turbans, often topped with a jeweled medallion.

Members of the Janissaries wore tall hats, while the sultans' bodyguards wore hats with tall, white plumes. We know about these modes of dress from illustrations, and from the magnificent robes preserved in the Topkapi Sarai in Istanbul.

▶ This caftan was worn by the Ottoman sultan Bayezid II.

The caftan is made from silk.

The sleeves are short.

There are buttons down to the waist.

Gold braid called "frogging" decorates the front.

The style of decoration of many Ottoman silks was similar to that found on ceramics such as tile panels.

Sinan (1489–1588)

Sinan was probably from a Greek family, but he became a Janissary in 1521 and went on to have a successful military career. He came to the notice of the sultan because of his work as a military engineer. In 1538 he was appointed court architect, a post he held until his death. During this time, he worked on more than 400 buildings, including the Topkapi Sarai, the Shehzade Mosque, and the Suleimaniye Mosque, all in Istanbul. Sinan was fascinated by the huge dome of the Byzantine cathedral of Saint Sophia in Istanbul, a building that was more than 1,000 years old. Under Muslim rule, Saint Sophia was converted into a mosque, but Sinan was determined to build a wider dome, and eventually succeeded. The dome of the Selimiye Mosque at Edirne, completed in 1575, spanned 102 feet (31 meters).

Ibn Sina (980–1037)

Known in the West as Avicenna, Ibn Sina was a talented child who had memorized the Qur'an by the age of ten. By the time he was seventeen, he was a well-known physician. He wrote more than 200 works on the sciences and philosophy, but his best-known work was the *al-Qanun fi at-Tibb (The Canon of Medicine)*. In these books, Ibn Sina summarized the practices of ancient Greek physicians such as Galen and Hippocrates, as well as describing his own experiments. He also listed more than 700 drugs sold by Islamic pharmacists, commenting on their use and effectiveness. *The Canon of Medicine* was translated into Latin in the 1100s and became the standard work of reference in both the Islamic and Western worlds for centuries after.

▶ This page is from Ibn Sina's *al-Qanun fi at-Tibb (The Canon of Medicine)*.

The astrolabe was used to show how the sky looked at a specific time and place.

The astrolabe is made from copper.

A map of the sky is drawn on the face of the astrolabe.

The rings were moved to set them to the correct positions.

Astronomy and cartography

Many Muslim rulers and scholars took a keen interest in astronomy. Several famous observatories were built across the Islamic world, including one in Samarkand, founded by the 15th-century Timurid ruler Ulugh Beg, and one in Istanbul, constructed in 1580. Observations of the stars were made using devices such as the **armillary sphere** and the astrolabe. There were no telescopes—these were invented in Europe in the 1600s. Instruments such as the astrolabe also helped with navigation. The land and sea trade networks that existed across and beyond the Islamic world encouraged the study of geography. One of the earliest maps of the known world was produced by an Arab named al-Idrisi (1100–1166), who studied at Córdoba. Mapmaking flourished in the 1500s under the Ottomans, mainly as a result of the Ottoman conquests.

◀ This astrolabe was made in Iraq in the 800s. Astrolabes were used to find the time during the day or night, to determine the time of events such as sunrise or sunset, and to find the positions of stars.

Religion

From the earliest times, the mosque provided the focus for every Islamic community. The first mosques were probably modeled on the house of the Prophet Muhammad ﷺ in Medina, used during his lifetime for prayer. The house was built around a square courtyard, with mud-brick walls. At the north and south ends, the trunks of palm trees supported a flat roof, giving some shelter from the sun. The design of mosques of the 600s at Basra and Kufa (both in Iraq) reflect this plan.

Women at prayer

The Iranian manuscript from the 1500s on page 37 shows a ruler and his courtiers attending prayer in a mosque. The women, veiled for modesty, are in a separate area. Women were allowed to pray in mosques in many, but not all, Muslim societies. There were separate areas for men and women to enter a mosque and to take part in *wudu,* the ritual washing before prayer. However, women were generally encouraged to say their prayers at home.

Minarets

In the time of Muhammad ﷺ, the *adhan* (call to prayer) was given from the roof of the Prophet's house. The **minaret** came into use after the Prophet's death, and the first examples were probably built in Syria or Egypt. A man called a *muezzin* called all Muslims to prayer from the minaret. The Great Mosque at Samarra had a conical minaret, but the more usual shape was a tall, slender, often highly decorated tower. Most mosques had one minaret, but some had multiple minarets—particularly the lavish mosques built in Istanbul under the **Ottomans**. The Suleimaniye Mosque has four minarets, while the mosque of Sultan Ahmed has six.

▼ This illustration is taken from an Iranian manuscript called *Majalis al-'Ushshaq* (*The Assemblies of the Lovers*). It dates from 1552.

The *minbar*

The Prophet Muhammad ﷺ delivered sermons to his followers from a simple pulpit—a high seat with three steps—situated in the shade of the southern side of the courtyard. From this developed the **minbar**, the pulpit situated to the right of the **mihrab** that became a feature of most mosques. The imam, the leader of communal prayer, delivered his Friday sermon from this place. In many cases, the *minbar* had three steps, like the one used by the Prophet ﷺ. But in many parts of the Islamic world, more elaborate versions came into use.

In the main area of the mosque, the men listen to a sermon.

This is the women's area of the mosque.

Small children sat with the women.

▼ This is the *qibla* wall in the Sultan Hasan mosque in Cairo, Egypt, built in the 1300s.

This mihrab *indicates the qibla (direction of prayer).*

This is the minbar.

The *mihrab*

In the early days at Medina, the Prophet Muhammad ﷺ and his followers faced towards Jerusalem while praying. But in 624, Muhammad ﷺ received a message from Allah instructing him to pray in the direction of Mecca in Saudi Arabia. Accordingly, prayers were said facing towards the south wall of the house. This became the **qibla**—the direction of Mecca to which Muslim prayer is always oriented. After Muhammad's death, the *qibla* came to be indicated in mosques by a niche called a **mihrab**. This became the focal point of the mosque, and was often highly decorated.

The Five Pillars

For Muslims, the teachings of Islam cover all aspects of life. These teachings include five special duties, often called the Five Pillars of Islam, that all Muslims must perform. They are: **shahada**, bearing witness; *salat*, prayer; *zakat*, religious tax; *sawm*, fasting; and *hajj*, pilgrimage. Since the time of Muhammad ﷺ, these duties have shaped everyday life for Muslims all over the world. Their importance is reflected in many aspects of Islamic art.

The *Shahada*

The words of the *Shahada* are, "*There is no god but Allah and Muhammad is the messenger of Allah.*" The use of the words of the *Shahada* as decorative calligraphic inscriptions was a constant reminder to Muslims of the importance of the message of Allah. The second half of the *Shahada* reminded Muslims that Muhammad ﷺ was the messenger of Allah, and that it was the message itself (and not the messenger) that was most important. This emphasis was reflected in the avoidance of images in Islamic sacred art.

▶ This prayer rug comes from Turkestan in central Asia. The design reflects the shape of a **mihrab**.

Friday mosques

Throughout the Islamic world, "Friday mosques" were built that were big enough to hold the congregation for the special Friday service. The Arabic word *masjid* (mosque) means "place of prostrations" (bowing down), and *salat* involves a particular ritual of movements and words that is performed on the floor. As a result, mosques have little furniture. Instead, Muslims often carry a small prayer carpet on which to carry out *salat*.

Salat and *zakat*

Muslims are required to pray five times a day, at set hours. They do not attend the mosque for all of these prayers, but midday prayers on Fridays are compulsory for all Muslim men. *Zakat* is a religious tax—through it, all Muslims give between 2.5 and 10 percent of their wealth or income to those who are less fortunate than themselves.

Sawm

During the month of Ramadan, Muslims observe a fast. For 30 days, they do not eat or drink during the hours of daylight. They recall the time that the Prophet Muhammad ﷺ received the first revelations from Allah. The end of this time of fasting is traditionally a time of celebration.

▶ This illustration is from the *Maqamah* of al-Hariri (see page 33). It shows celebrations at the end of Ramadan.

The flags bear religious inscriptions.

Two men are blowing into long trumpets.

Two kettle drums are mounted on a horse's back.

This pilgrim is touching the black stone that is set into the side of the Ka'ba.

The Ka'ba was later covered with a black cloth, called the kiswah.

The pilgrims wear special clothes, each made from two pieces of white cloth.

Hajj

The *hajj* is the pilgrimage to Mecca that every Muslim must try to undertake once in his or her lifetime. The origin of the *hajj* is the pilgrimage made by the Prophet Muhammad ﷺ from Medina to Mecca a short time before his death. In the early Islamic world, *hajj* caravans were organized from the cities of Cairo, Damascus, and Baghdad.

These caravans were very profitable for the traders who organized them, and for the nomadic peoples of the Arabian desert, where the caravans passed on their way to Mecca. Thousands of people traveled with these caravans, and it took great organization to supply them with water and food for the journey through the desert. Such a huge and regular movement of people from all corners of the Islamic world encouraged the interchange and mixing of ideas, as well as promoting trade among the peoples.

◀ This painting from the 1400s shows pilgrims around the **Ka'ba** in Mecca. Circling the Ka'ba is an important part of the *hajj*. The illustration comes from a book about religious observance.

The Qur'an

The **Qur'an** is the sacred book of all Muslims. It contains the revelations from Allah given to the Prophet Muhammad ﷺ by the angel Jibril (Gabriel). The revelations were collected in a written version after the death of Muhammad ﷺ to form the Qur'an. Muslims believe that the Qur'an is the word of Allah, and that not one single word was added or changed by Muhammad ﷺ.

The earliest Qur'ans

The Prophet Muhammad ﷺ learned each revelation by heart as it was revealed to him (*Qur'an* means "recitation" in Arabic). The revelations were later written down on a variety of materials—sheep bones, pieces of pottery, and bits of leather. Muhammad ﷺ also taught the revelations to his followers, and had them recited during worship.

A person who knew the complete text of the Qur'an was known as a *hafiz* (plural: *huffaz*). After the death of the Prophet ﷺ, the first **caliph**, Abu Bakr ﷺ, assembled the *huffaz* and ordered a complete written version of the Qur'an to be made in one book. During the time of the third caliph, Uthman ﷺ, all other versions were checked against this text and any that differed were destroyed. Many copies were made of the standard text, and sent to cities all over the Islamic world. Today, just two survive—one in Tashkent in Uzbekistan, and one in Istanbul.

▼This Qur'an dates from the 800s or 900s. The words are written in **kufic** script (see page 42). The Qur'an is made from vellum.

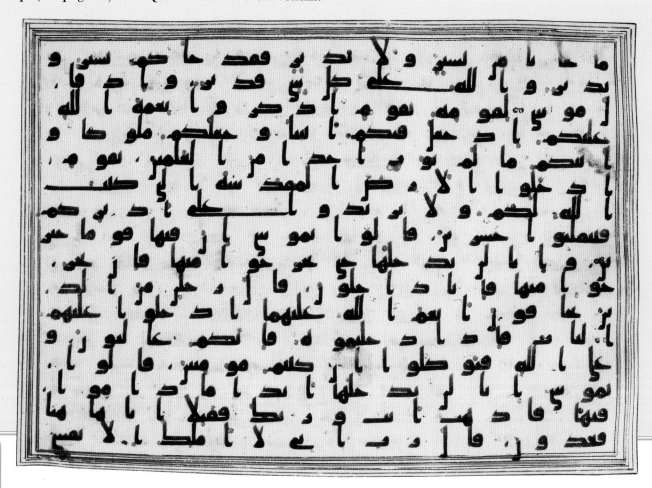

The impact of the Qur'an

The words of the Qur'an are at the heart of the Islamic faith. Copying the Qur'an was an act of worship practiced by male and female Muslims through the centuries, in all parts of the Islamic world. The letters on the page were made as beautiful as possible in order to be worthy of the divine words being written. This art is known as **calligraphy**. The words of the Qur'an were frequently used to decorate the surfaces of buildings such as mosques, tombs, and *madrasahs*, as well as mosque furniture such as lamps.

The art of the Qur'an

In keeping with Islamic tradition, the Qur'an was not illustrated with any images. However, many richly decorated Qur'ans were produced in all parts of the Islamic world. In Egypt, the Mamluks (former Turkish slaves who founded a dynasty in Egypt and Syria between 1250 and 1517) were renowned for the lavish and beautiful Qur'ans they produced. In particular, three Qur'ans copied for Sultan Shaban II (reigned 1363–1376) in *muhaqqaq* script are notable for the refined and detailed quality of the work.

▶ This glass mosque lamp was made in Egypt in the 1300s. The oil inside was lit and the lamp was then hung from the ceiling of the mosque by metal chains.

The glass is decorated with enamel and gold.

The bottom part of the inscription says, "Glory to the sultan our lord." The other side has his name, al-Malik al-Nasir Muhammad.

Muslims have 99 names for God. The inscriptions show some of the 99 names.

The lamp is covered in calligraphic inscriptions.

The inscriptions are in thuluth *script*.

The metal chains to hang the lamp were attached to these handles.

Calligraphy

The highest of all the Islamic arts is **calligraphy**—the art of beautiful writing. The importance of calligraphy stemmed from the Muslim belief that the **Qur'an** is the literal word of Allah. Schools of calligraphy were established throughout the Islamic world, and both men and women became accomplished and famous scribes.

Styles of calligraphy

Arabic script is written and read from right to left. It is a Semitic script, in the same family as Hebrew and Ethiopic. Its origins lie in the script of the Nabataeans, **nomads** who established a kingdom with its capital at Petra (in modern-day Jordan) in the late 600s and early 500s **B.C.E.** As schools of calligraphy were established through the Islamic world, different styles of writing emerged. The two oldest styles were *kufic* (named after the town of Kufa, an early center of calligraphy) and *naskhi*. *Kufic* was an angular script, well-suited to surface decoration in stone and mosaic. It was also used for early Qur'ans. *Naskhi* was a more flowing style, used also for secular writing.

As styles of calligraphy became more refined, they also became more varied. Different types of *kufic* and *naskhi* scripts were developed. For example, Eastern *kufic* was an elegant and refined angular script, while six flowing scripts became the classical scripts of Islamic calligraphy—*naskhi, thuluth, muhaqqaq, rayhani, riqa,* and *tauqi.*

▲ This Mughal painting shows a scribe (right) and a painter at work.

Ibn al-Bawwab

Ibn al-Bawwab (d.1022) was one of the most famous calligraphers at the **Abbasid** court in Baghdad. He learned his art from the daughter of another famous calligrapher, Ibn Muqla, who worked at the Abbasid court at the beginning of the 900s. Ibn Muqla was responsible for developing the classical scripts of Islamic calligraphy. Ibn al-Bawwab is said to have known the Qur'an by heart, and to have copied it 64 times during his lifetime. However, only one copy is known to have survived.

▲ The inscriptions around the Dome of the Rock in Jerusalem are written in giant *kufic* script.

The headings are in the ornamental thuluth script.

The main body of the text is in naskhi script.

The script is read from right to left.

◀ This Qur'an was copied by Ibn al-Bawwab. It is the earliest surviving Qur'an to be written in *naskhi* script on paper. Earlier Qur'ans were usually written on vellum, a type of parchment made from animal skin.

Timeline

c.570
Muhammad ﷺ is born.

610
Muhammad ﷺ receives first messages from the angel Jibril (Gabriel).

622
The *hijra* (migration to Medina) occurs.

632
Muhammad ﷺ dies; Abu Bakr ﷺ becomes **caliph**.

634
Abu Bakr ﷺ dies; Umar ﷺ becomes caliph.

634–644
Muslim armies invade Syria, Egypt, and Iraq.

638
Muslim armies capture Jerusalem.

644
Umar ﷺ is assassinated, and Uthman ﷺ becomes caliph.

644–650
Muslim armies invade Iran and Afghanistan and move into North Africa.

656
Uthman ﷺ is assassinated; Ali ﷺ becomes caliph.

661
Ali ﷺ is assassinated; Mu'awiya I founds **Umayyad** Dynasty.

685
Work starts on the Dome of the Rock in Jerusalem.

705
Work starts on the Great Mosque in Damascus.

750
Abbasids seize power from Umayyads.

756
Abd al-Rahman defeats Abbasid ruler and establishes al-Andalus in southern Spain.

762–773
Baghdad founded as capital of Abbasid Empire.

784
Work starts on the Great Mosque of Córdoba.

c.836
Abbasids move their capital from Baghdad to Samarra.

892
Abbasid capital returns to Baghdad.

969
Fatimids defeat Abbasids in Egypt.

973
Fatimids establish capital at Cairo.

990s
Seljuk Turks convert to Islam.

1055
Seljuk sultan Tughril-beg takes over Baghdad.

1169
Saladin seizes power in Egypt.

1171
Saladin proclaims return to **Sunni** Islam in Egypt.

1206
Mongols form confederation of tribes under leader Genghis Khan.

1258
Mongols sack Baghdad and bring Abbasid rule to an end.

1380s–1405
Timur establishes control over much of Central Asia, Iran, and Iraq.

1453
Ottomans capture Constantinople and rename it Istanbul.

1492
Granada, the last Muslim stronghold in Spain, is captured by the troops of the Catholic monarchs, Ferdinand and Isabella.

1501
Safavids capture Tabriz and found their empire.

1520–66
Ottoman sultan Suleiman "the Magnificent" reigns.

1526–30
First Mughal emperor, Babur, reigns.

1556–1605
Mughal emperor Akbar the Great reigns.

1588–1629
Safavid Shah Abbas the Great reigns.

1597
Work starts on new Safavid capital at Isfahan.

1627–1658
Mughal emperor Shah Jahan reigns.

Glossary

Abbasid the name of the dynasty that held the title of caliph from 750 until 1258

adhan the call to prayer

Almohad a person from North Africa; the Almohads defeated the Almoravids for control of al-Andalus in 1147

Almoravid a person from the western Sahara; the Amoravids took control of al-Andalus in the 1000s

armillary sphere a large wooden astronomical instrument used to plot the orbits of stars and planets

bazaar a covered marketplace, usually containing many small shops

B.C.E. "before the common era"—used to indicated dates before the birth of Jesus Christ

Berber a native inhabitant of North Africa

Byzantine a person from the empire of Byzantium, the eastern Roman Empire

caliph (successor) a title given to the successors of the Prophet Muhammad ﷺ

calligraphy the art of beautiful handwriting

caravanserai a medieval inn on a trade route

C.E. "of the common era"—after the birth of Jesus Christ

Fatimid the name of the dynasty that ruled in North Africa and Egypt from 969 until 1171

harem the women's quarters in a Muslim home

iwan a vaulted, open-air hall

Ka'ba the cube-shaped structure in Mecca toward which all Muslims direct their prayer

kufic a type of angular Arabic script, named after the town of Kufa in Iraq

luster a type of glaze that contains a metallic pigment

madrasah an Islamic college

mausoleum a large and grand tomb

mihrab a niche in the wall of a mosque that indicates the direction of prayer

minaret the tower from which a muezzin issues the *adhan*

minbar the pulpit in a mosque from where the address or sermon is given during Friday prayers

Mongol a nomadic person from central Asia; they formed an empire in the 1200s

Mughal name of the dynasty of Muslim emperors who ruled India from 1526 to 1857

naskhi type of Arabic script with a flowing style

Night of Ascent according to Muslim belief, the night when the Prophet Muhammad ﷺ ascended from a rock on the Temple Mount in Jerusalem into the heavens

nomad a member of a people that roams from place to place to find fresh pasture for their animals

Ottoman the name of the dynasty of Turkish sultans who ruled Anatolia and much of the Mediterranean and the Middle East from the 1300s until 1922

pigment a substance that gives something color

qibla the direction of prayer for all Muslims, facing toward the city of Mecca

Qur'an the sacred book of Islam. Muslims believe that the Qur'an is the literal word of Allah, as given to the Prophet Muhammad ﷺ in the messages delivered by the angel Jibril.

Rashidun "rightly guided ones," the first four caliphs who held power after the death of the Prophet Muhammad ﷺ: Abu Bakr (632–634), Umar (634–644), Uthman (644–656), and Ali (656–661) [Peace Be Upon Them].

Safavid name of the dynasty of Shi'ite Muslims who ruled Iran from 1501 to 1736

Sassanian Persian Empire ruling from 224 C.E. until its defeat by the Muslim armies in 651

Seljuk a Turkish nomad from Central Asia; they converted to Islam in the 990s and seized power from the Abbasids in the 1000s

Shahada the Muslim declaration of faith: "There is no god but Allah, and Muhammad is the messenger of Allah."

Shi'ite a Muslim who believes that leadership of the Islamic community passed directly to Ali ﷺ, as the closest blood relative of the Prophet Muhammad ﷺ, and then through Ali's descendants

Sunnah the model practices, customs, and traditions of the Prophet Muhammad ﷺ

Sunni Muslim who believes in the successorship of the first four caliphs (the *Rashidun*)

Umayyad first Islamic Dynasty, ruling from 661 until 750

Uzbek Turkish Mongol tribe that converted to Islam in the 1300s

wudu ritual washing before prayer

Further Reading

Ali, Daud, et al. *Great Civilizations of the East*. New York: Anness Publishing, 2003.

Beardwood, Mary. *Children's Encyclopedia of Arabia*. Northampton, Mass.: Interlink, 2002.

Belloli, Andrea. *Exploring World Art*. Los Angeles: Getty Publications, 1999.

Cheshire, Gerard, and Paula Hammond. *Cultures and Costumes: The Middle East*. Broomall, Penn.: Mason Crest, 2002.

Hipps, Amelia. *Islam, Christianity, Judaism*. Broomall, Penn.: Mason Crest, 2003.

Hodges, Rick. *What Muslims Think, How They Live*. Broomall, Penn.: Mason Crest, 2003.

Hunter, Erica, and Mike Corbishley. *First Civilizations*. New York: Facts on File, 2003.

Knight, Judson. *Ancient Civilizations*. Farmington Hills, Mich.: Gale Group, 2000.

Kort, Michael. *The Handbook of the Middle East*. Brookfield, Conn.: Millbrook Press, 2002.

Kotapish, Dawn. *Daily Life in Ancient and Modern Baghdad*. Minneapolis, Minn.: Lerner Publishing, 2000.

Martell, Hazel Mary. *The World of Islam Before 1700*. Chicago: Raintree, 1999.

Nardo, Don. *Empires of Mesopotamia*. Farmington Hills, Mich.: Gale Group, 2001.

Uecker, Jeffry. *History Through Art Timeline*. Worcester, Mass.: Davis Publishers, 2001.

Wilkinson, Philip. *Islam*. New York: Dorling Kindersley, 2002.

Woods, Mary B., and Michael Woods. *Ancient Construction*. Minneapolis, Minn.: Lerner Publishing, 2000.

Index